Fangs
BLACK MAMBAS

Sudden Death!

by Nancy White

Consultant: Raoul Bain, Biodiversity Specialist, Herpetology
Center for Biodiversity and Conservation
American Museum of Natural History
New York, New York

BEARPORT
PUBLISHING

New York, New York

Credits

Cover and Title Page, © Maik Dobiey/Bruce Coleman/Photoshot; TOC, © Brian Kenney/Oxford Scientific; 5, © Maik Dobiey/Bruce Coleman/Photoshot; 6, © David Bygott; 7, © Anthony Bannister/Animals Animals/Photolibrary; 8, © Lynn M. Stone/Nature Picture Library; 9, © Photocyclops/SuperStock; 10, © Maik Dobiey/Bruce Coleman/Photoshot; 11, © Lynn M. Stone/Animals Animals Enterprises; 12, © Johan Marais; 13, © Maik Dobiey/Bruce Coleman/Photoshot; 14, © Brian Kenney/Oxford Scientific; 15, © Maik Dobiey/Bruce Coleman/Photoshot; 16, © Günter Leitenbauer; 17, © Johan van Renslourg; 18, © Maik Dobiey/Bruce Coleman/Photoshot; 19, © Maik Dobiey/Bruce Coleman/Photoshot; 20, © Adrian Warren/Ardea; 21, © Paul Freed/Animals Animals Enterprises; 22, © Günter Leitenbauer; 23A, © Snowleopard1/Shutterstock; 23B, © Susan Flashman/Shuttterstock; 23C, © iconex/Shutterstock; 23D, © Maria Dryfhout/Shutterstock; 23E, © Snowleopard1/Shutterstock; 23F, © Photocyclops/SuperStock; 23G, © R. Andrew Odum/Peter Arnold, Inc./Alamy.

Publisher: Kenn Goin
Senior Editor: Lisa Wiseman
Creative Director: Spencer Brinker
Photo Researcher: Q2A Media: Poulomi Basu
Design: Dawn Beard Creative

Library of Congress Cataloging-in-Publication Data

White, Nancy, 1942–
  Black mambas : sudden death! / by Nancy White.
    p. cm. (Fangs)
  Includes bibliographical references and index.
  ISBN-13: 978-1-59716-766-6 (library binding)
  ISBN-10: 1-59716-766-5 (library binding)
  1. Black mamba—Juvenile literature. I. Title.

QL666.O64W445 2009
597.96'4—dc22

                          2008039892

For more information, write to Bearport Publishing Company, Inc., 101 Fifth Avenue, Suite 6R, New York, New York 10003. Printed in the United States of America.

10 9 8 7 6 5 4 3 2 1

Contents

A Fast Killer

Through the hot African forest, a slender snake slithers along the ground. It holds its head high above the forest floor as it searches for something to eat. Suddenly, it spots some hikers and hides behind a rock. The hikers, unaware of the danger, walk too close to the rock. The scared snake hisses loudly, spreads its narrow **hood**, and flicks its forked tongue in and out. Then, with lightning speed, it **strikes** and bites one of them on the head.

A bite from this snake, a black mamba, is one of the deadliest in the world. Within minutes, the hiker's head swells and he's unable to see or talk. Without special medicine, he'll die within as little as 15 minutes.

Black mambas are the world's fastest snakes, slithering at speeds of up to 12.5 miles per hour (20 kph). They live in parts of central and southern Africa. They can usually be found moving over grassy or rocky ground and through low tree branches.

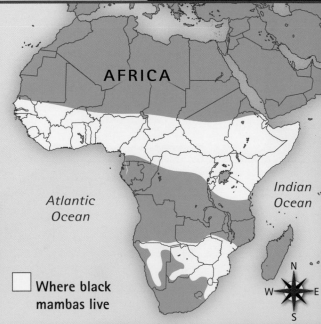

AFRICA

Atlantic Ocean

Indian Ocean

☐ Where black mambas live

N W E S

A black mamba

The Killer's Colors

The black mamba is actually not black. Its body can be brown, gray, or dark green. The word *black* in the snake's name refers to the color inside its mouth. This purplish black can easily be seen when the snake opens its mouth to hiss.

The black mamba's body colors blend in with the surroundings when the snake is on the ground. When in a tree, its long, thin body looks like a branch. Blending in helps the black mamba stay hidden from its enemies and sneak up on its **prey**.

black mouth

The black mamba is the largest snake in Africa. Most adults are 8 to 10 feet (2.4 to 3 m) long. The biggest one found, however, measured 14 feet (4.2 m). The black mamba's body, though, is very thin—only about the width of an adult's thumb.

100 Percent Deadly

The black mamba is not only long and fast, it's also deadly. Only two drops of **venom** are needed to kill a human. Once bitten, death is 100 percent certain, unless the person is quickly injected with a special medicine made from black mamba venom.

This deadly snake is quick to attack when it's frightened by an animal or a person. When it strikes at a human, it often aims for the head or chest. It rarely misses. Luckily, this dangerous snake is shy. It would rather slither down a hole than attack a person.

A green mamba

There are three other types of mambas in Africa. They are bright green. The insides of their mouths are white. These green mambas are smaller and more timid than black mambas.

A black mamba
about to attack

At Home in a Hole

Black mambas are so shy that they spend much of their time hiding in holes made by other animals, either in the ground or in hollow trees. Unlike most snakes, a black mamba goes back to the same hole every day for years. It also sleeps in its hole at night. It comes out during the day to hunt.

When black mambas are not hiding, hunting, or sleeping, they like to sunbathe on rocks or tree branches. They often have favorite sunning spots, which they return to each day.

A black mamba inside a hollow tree

Like all snakes, black mambas
depend on the heat of the sun to
keep their bodies warm. This is why
they need to spend time out in the open,
where the sun can reach them. If they
get too hot, they go back into a hole.

Senses for Survival

When a black mamba hunts for prey, it uses all of its senses. It sees better than most snakes and is especially good at sensing motion. If an animal moves in the grass, the snake will spot it immediately. Bones in the snake's lower jaw also detect motion. They feel the ground shaking when something is moving nearby. Like other snakes, the black mamba uses both its nostrils and forked tongue to smell the air for the scent of prey.

▲ Black mambas have very large eyes.

forked tongue

When a black mamba flicks out its tongue, it picks up tiny scent particles from the air. When it pulls its tongue back in, these particles touch the roof of its mouth. From there, a message goes to the snake's brain, which can tell what the smell is and where it's coming from.

Killer on the Move

When searching for prey, the black mamba slithers quickly over the ground or along tree branches, flicking out its tongue. The snake keeps its head raised up to 1.5 feet (45 cm) off the ground as it moves. This helps it look for small animals, such as squirrels or rats.

After the deadly hunter spots its prey, it usually stays still and waits for the animal to come near. Sometimes it slowly sneaks up on its prey. Then it raises its head even higher and strikes out with lightning speed, biting the animal with its sharp **fangs**.

▲ A black mamba keeps its head high off the ground when looking for food.

This killer strikes with tremendous force. A black mamba that is 12 feet (3.6 m) long can lunge out and bite an animal that is 6 feet (1.8 m) away—that's half the snake's body length.

The Death Bite

Once a **victim** has been bitten, the snake usually lets it go. The prey may try to run away, but it won't get far. Why? The black mamba's powerful venom will kill it within minutes.

At first, the venom stops the victim's muscles from working. Since lungs are controlled by muscles, they stop working, too. Unable to breathe, the animal dies. Then the snake uses its keen sense of smell to find where the dead prey has fallen.

fangs

▲ Black mambas have short fangs.

When a black mamba bites a bird, the snake holds on until the animal stops moving. Otherwise, the bird might fly away and travel too far for the snake to find it before it dies.

Jaws Wide Open

When the black mamba finds its lifeless victim, the hungry hunter grabs the animal's head in its jaws and devours it whole. How does the black mamba eat an animal that's bigger than its head? Like most snakes, its mouth can open very wide because its upper and lower jaws are loosely connected.

Even before the prey is swallowed, a special liquid inside the black mamba's mouth starts digesting the victim. When the animal reaches the snake's stomach, it is completely digested there, bones and all.

▲ A black mamba starting to eat a rodent

A black mamba almost finished swallowing its meal

Black mambas are often ready to kill and eat again a few days after a meal.

Little Killers

In the spring, black mambas mate and the female lays 6 to 20 eggs. Then she leaves her eggs and never comes back. About three months later, the eggs hatch.

The babies are less than two feet (61 cm) long at birth. They grow fast, however. By the age of one, they may be six feet (1.8 m) long. The young snakes are smaller and lighter in color than fully grown black mambas. Otherwise, they are just like their parents—fast and dangerous, with enough deadly poison to kill almost any animal they bite.

Sometimes two male black mambas fight over a female. The two males rise up and wrap themselves around each other. They don't try to bite, however. Instead, they try to push each other down to the ground. The bigger, stronger snake wins.

▲ Two male black mambas fighting over a female black mamba

A newly hatched black mamba ready to strike

Fang Facts

- The black mamba is different than most other snakes because it will bite its victim more than once when attacking.

- Many venomous snakes don't use venom when they bite humans. They save their poison for killing prey. A black mamba's bite, however, is almost always venomous.

- A black mamba's bite doesn't have to be deep to kill a person. Anyone who is even scratched by the snake's fangs needs to get medical help immediately.

- Black mambas and their relatives, such as king cobras and coral snakes, don't have very long fangs. If their fangs were longer, they would bite themselves when they closed their mouths!

- Black mambas often lose one or both of their fangs. Like other venomous snakes, they soon grow new fangs to replace the lost ones.

- A person who meets up with a black mamba should stand very still. There's a good chance that the snake will go away. It will, however, strike at anything that moves.

Glossary

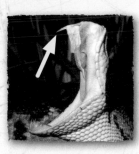

fangs (FANGZ) long pointy teeth

venom (VEN-uhm) poison made by some snakes

hood (HOOD) skin that some snakes spread behind their heads to make themselves look bigger

victim (VIK-tuhm) an animal that is attacked or killed by another animal

prey (PRAY) animals that are hunted and eaten by other animals

strikes (STRIKES) hits or attacks something

Index

Read More

Fiedler, Julie. *Mambas.* New York: The Rosen Publishing Group (2008).

Klein, Adam G. *Black Mambas.* Edina, MN: ABDO Publishing Company (2006).

Richardson, Adele D. *Mambas.* Mankato, MN: Capstone Press (2004).

Learn More Online

To learn more about black mambas, visit
www.bearportpublishing.com/Fangs

About the Author

Nancy White has written many science and nature books
for children. She lives in a small town near New York City,
in the Hudson River Valley.